Million Dollar Days

Million Dollar Days

What If You Were Given a Million Dollars for Just One Day?

Maryanna Young

Foreword by Kim Fletcher

Million Dollar Days
What If You Were Given A Million Dollars for Just One More Day?
Maryanna Young © 2018

Print ISBN: 978-1-61206-176-4
eBook ISBN: 978-1-61206-177-1
Audio Book ISBN: 978-1-61206-178-8

Cover Design Concept: Marina Alcoser
Cover and Interior Design: Fusion Creative Works, FusionCW.com
Lead Editor: Jennifer Regner

For more information, email the author at maryannayoung@gmail.com

Published by

ALOHA
PUBLISHING

AlohaPublishing.com
Printed in the United States of America

To anyone who may have forgotten that
time spent with significant people in your
life is beyond what money can buy.

"Measure *wealth* not by the things you *have*, but by the things you have for which you would not take *money*."

Foreword

By Kim Fletcher

One of my favorite lines from the book you are about to read simply states, "Mary Oppel dressed, prayed, and lived to be ready for anything."

This book is a simple, one-cup-of-coffee read, and yet it holds the potential to ignite you to rethink your perspective on how you invest your time.

The lessons we learn through life, love, struggle, and grief help us reframe true wealth regardless of our net worth.

When most people think of legacy, they think of that which is left behind at the time of someone's death. You will soon realize that the most powerful gift you can give to your family and friends is what you invest in them day to day in the form of a living legacy.

What will you do with the day in front of you? Would it change the way you value and invest it if you truly believed it was worth a million dollars?

Million Dollar Days will awaken you to the hidden value of your greatest assets—your time and relationships.

Million Dollar Days

Who in your life do you credit with teaching you to value and make the most of every day?

For me, that person is my maternal grandmother, Mary Oppel. She was more than a grandparent. Looking back, she was a constant driving force in my life—someone who influenced me far more than I realized. Like a master architect, Grandma O passed along a blueprint for living a life of freedom and significance. I am still using that blueprint into my fifth decade of life.

Mary Oppel was ahead of her time in many ways. In fact, I believe that God made her uniquely timeless in order to influence multiple and future generations through her life.

In our fast-paced culture, a person's legacy can get lost or overshadowed all too quickly, which is why I wrote this short piece. I am sharing a portion of her story because I want to share her heart for the generations. My hope is to see many lives tap into the blueprint that made her life a lasting blessing with a ripple effect that is ever growing. Picture relay runners getting ready to grab the baton to take their lap.

If you are reading this story, it is your turn to take the baton and run your lap with excellence.

The Lady With the Signature Style

I want to give you a glimpse into the life and signature style of Mary Oppel. My grandmother was a beautiful, funny, athletic, straight-to-the-point woman. She was a magnificent mix of elegance and faith. She never left home without being dressed as if headed to a special event. She also never left home without taking time to read her Bible. Always color coordinated and with perfectly styled hair, Grandma O dressed, prayed, and lived to be ready for anything.

For years, especially when traveling, I enjoyed being among the best-dressed in the airport. I can now see that this simple practice was instilled in me out of my own longing to be more like this amazing woman.

Far more important than my clothing, I also learned early on to keep my Bible close at hand. I could never thank my grandmother enough for all she did to instill faith into my early life, equipping me to make God and His Word integral parts of my daily life. Mary Oppel didn't stop at attending church. She lived her faith daily with more care than she used to choose her outfit or style her hair.

If you are picturing a stuffy church lady, think again. This woman was uber cool and spontaneous. Children, teens, and adults loved being around her. She elevated the meaning of grace, beauty, strength, and fun to new levels for me and for many others.

One of my fondest memories of Grandma O was watching her complete a 5K (3.1 mile) race when she was 84. She finished that race in just under 40 minutes—for someone who was a walker more than a runner, that's remarkable. A short year and a half later, she would finish her race of life.

The Day My World Changed

For the final five years of her life, I was blessed that we lived together in my home. Grandma O was fully capable of living alone, but she loved people. My grandfather had passed away after 59 years of marriage, leaving her wanting to be surrounded by those she loved.

When she first decided to move in with me, I lived in an 800-square-foot house I owned at the time in Boise's North End. This one bedroom, one bath house was a bit shy of the space my grandmother wanted for hospitality and hosting out-of-town company. I had to laugh one day when her strength and spontaneity collided with her desire for more space. She insisted it was time to move, as she began to coach me on the most cost-effective way to make our own FOR SALE sign that we would hammer into our front lawn. Before she could say *pack your bags* I had purchased the house of her dreams, complete with more than enough square footage and a master suite with a pink vanity and mauve-colored kitchen counter. She quickly laid claim to the large lower floor bedroom while I had more than enough space upstairs with a loft and a sunroom. I cringed at the countertops, but I loved her more.

Those were five of the greatest years of my life, although I don't know if I recognized it at the time.

Grandma O enjoyed amazing health in despite of recovering from a complicated heart surgery with seven bypasses and a replacement aorta value, the year she came to live with me. This warrior of a woman bounced back and continued to travel extensively to visit family and friends in various locations, nationally and internationally.

While I shared many great times with my grandmother in those days, I also came away with regrets that have been challenging to overcome.

I was a driven young professional and can admit now that I often placed a higher priority on work and accomplishment than on my key relationships.

I cannot tell you how much I have wished that I could return to those days and hit the reset button on life. I would have taken time to stop and enjoy many of the moments that I took for granted. I was living as if our days together were endless. Then something devastating rocked my world—my healthy, vivacious grandmother passed away suddenly from a brain aneurysm.

Her final day of life was spent doing her favorite things. She read her Bible, took a short walk in the neighborhood, and later cooked dinner for us to share. Just a few short days before, she had remarked: "I feel so good, I am sure I will live another 10 years."

The hope of another 10 years vanished in the hours that followed that evening. I was left with my own world turned upside down. I am sure you can recall a moment when you felt blindsided and keenly aware that life was about to change forever. If so, you can relate to how I felt at the time.

I was numb, shaken, and confused. Immediately, I wanted to turn back time. My own life flashed before me, including the years shared with Grandma O. I felt as if I was watching a time-lapsed video. Memories of times shared and times I had failed to be present flooded my mind and heart in a relentless barrage of emotion. In an instant, I began to take stock of everything in my life.

The Moment of Truth

It then occurred to me that I had just experienced the most profound *moment of truth* up to this point in my own life. While her life had impacted me daily, it was her death that changed me completely. The magnitude of the loss I felt was nearly paralyzing.

Before you read any further, consider what I now know to be true. Take stock of your priorities and how you are investing your time, energy, and resources while there is still time.

This moment of desperation led me to cry out to God, pleading—**"If only I could have one more day with Grandma O. I would give a million dollars."** As quickly as the words left my mouth, I felt God imprint His gentle reply on my heart as He spoke, "Don't worry. Your grandmother is with me. Now you can have *million dollar days* with the people around you." That assurance and its implied challenge brought an understanding that immediately began to change the way I lived day to day.

When I would find myself wishing I could intention-ally take time to share one more cup of her favorite peppermint tea or cook one more meal together, I would take another step toward restructuring my days. I shifted my work schedule in order to focus more time and energy into the relationships I had been blessed with.

I wanted to live as if every day was actually worth one million dollars. I understood at a deeper level that it was up to me to steward my time and resources well. I was left longing to honor God and my grandmother by the way I crafted and spent my days.

One of her favorite passages of scripture was Psalm 37:4-5, which says: "Take delight in the Lord, and he will give you your heart's desires. Commit everything you do to the Lord. Trust him, and he will help you" (NLT). I had never been more aware of how much I needed God's help than during this restructuring.

I wanted to learn to love more, listen more, laugh more, forgive more, and hug more. I had watched God's love flow effortlessly through my grandmother and I wanted to continue that legacy of love. The coming months and years were filled with numerous steps of healing as I allowed God to unravel well-worn patterns of perfectionism and performance that had marked my driven personality.

Slowly and profoundly, I became empowered to elevate people and relationships over professional pursuits. My focus shifted, and my life expanded.

Mary Oppel loved to spend time with family and friends and often took long trips with them. Relationships were always her priority. One thing I began doing to follow in her footsteps was taking significant trips with people as God would highlight them. It might be a niece or nephew planning for their futures. It might be a friend who lacked the resources to travel on their own but was in desperate need of a vacation. It might be simply unplugging alone to allow me to listen to God and take stock of my life.

My grandmother instilled in me that life can be great even in the midst of challenging circumstances. Among her losses were four of her own children and her beloved husband of 59 years.

How did she remain so joyful in the midst of such great loss in her life? That is only one of the hundreds of unanswered questions I now have because I failed to take the time to ask and really listen.

My own *to do* list feels longer today than ever before. Yours may too. If we are not mindful, the urgent will crowd out the important things in life. Take it from me. Identify your priorities and guard them with your life.

Priorities Without a Price

I personally have known and worked with many wealthy individuals who will tell you that the *life they love* is not found in making money as a priority. The best of life is made up of the moments that can never be recaptured, such as the expression on a child's face when they see you on the bench cheering at their first game or merely taking the day off to do something that is extremely meaningful to them and to you. These are the moments that are worth a million dollars in your life and in the lives of those you choose to support.

If you feel regret over lost moments, allow that emotion to act as a catalyst that propels you toward positive growth. It is too late for me to recapture moments with my grandmother, but it is never too late for me to live out her legacy as I invest in those around me.

Perhaps it is time to leave work early to attend those games. It may be time to plan a trip with that special person you need to reconnect with—and timing is everything. It may mean leaving a card on your co-worker's desk reminding them that you see and appreciate them. It may be that you need to embrace and begin to pass on this Million Dollar Days lifestyle to those in your personal and professional circle.

Our lives were designed to have a continual ripple effect. We must decide if that ripple will be positive or negative. Dollars cannot buy what only the heart possesses. Kindness, love, value, and presence are gifts that the truly wealthy at heart know how to give freely. In fact, the heart is amazing as the gifts given from this deeply personal place multiply each time you give them away.

My spontaneous grandmother loved to travel. One year before she passed away, we traveled to New Zealand for three weeks. In those weeks together, we stayed overnight at four local farms, toured Dunedin Castle, visited a French mansion, and took a boat trip to stay three nights on Stewart Island. She wanted to spend Christmas week there, and so we did.

Only 10 days before her death, I flew with her to visit friends and family in Oregon. On the way there, we stopped for an early breakfast while we waited for a favorite shoe store to open. If you knew Grandma O in her later years, shopping for fashionable and functional Nine West shoes was a real delight for her. After leaving the store and while still satisfied from breakfast, we approached Multnomah Falls. She had remembered a restaurant with windows that were continually drenched by the flow of an overhead waterfall. Of course she wanted to take time to visit that restaurant. My practical side reminded her that we already had breakfast, but her spontaneous side overrode my decision to keep going because she knew how to celebrate and slow down. So there we were—still completely full, we ate a second breakfast while listening to the roar of the falls, watching as they washed over us.

Just as the waterfall seemed to tumble over our table, let the refreshing perspective of Grandma O wash over your life.

What needs to be washed away? Have you forgotten how to stop and celebrate? Is life moving so quickly that those around you feel they can never capture your full attention? Does your computer and phone ever get silenced long enough to hear the heart of that friend or family member who really needs to know that you are willing to be present with them?

On that same trip to Multnomah Falls, I recall a moment when her humor stopped me in my tracks. We watched a man and his Dachshund wiener dog walk by, and Grandma O simply and quietly remarked, "Somebody told that guy to get a long little doggy . . . and he did."

I laughed out loud! Today, that laughter has turned into a transforming life lesson. My life moved so quickly before her death that I would never have noticed. Even if I had noticed a guy and a dog, I would never have taken time to see the humor embedded in that moment.

How You Live Matters

I once had the audacity to ask God for one more million-dollar day, but today I realize that He had already given me more than I could ever steward in the moments my grandmother and I shared, and in the life lessons she imprinted on my heart.

You may or may not have someone this amazing and precious in your life. If you do, value them while you can. If you do not, never forget you may be called to be that person yourself. You can always give to the world what you wish you possessed. Be on the lookout . . . the baton of life is being passed along. Don't drop it! The race is your life and how you run it matters more than you may imagine.

We did not complete our final 5K together in a record-setting time, but it is among my fondest memories. While our finish time was insignificant, it feels as if Mary Oppel finished her life far too quickly.

In II Timothy 4:7, Paul writes, "I have fought the good fight, I have finished the race, and I have remained faithful" (NLT).

Life is different than a race. It's not the fastest runner who gets the prize, but the one wise enough to slow down, value life along the way, and even stop to help fellow runners. The prize goes to the one who remains faithful to God and to the people entrusted to our care. In a 5K, there is only one winner, but every person who lives the way Grandma O did is reaping their own rewards. Our ultimate reward awaits us in Heaven, but I have learned that there is also Heaven on Earth when we learn to make every day a million dollar day.

Acknowledgments

Mahalo nui loa (thank you very much in Hawaiian) to Kim Fletcher for rewriting the original version of *Million Dollar Days* that appeared in the book she co-authored, *Your Exceptional Life Begins Now*. Your insight was great on a very personal story.

Many thanks to my friends, whom Grandma O would have loved, who read and added their insights to this story: Jennifer Regner, Anna McHargue, and Amy Hoppock.

Thanks to Marina Alcoser for creative content on the cover as well as my wonderful team of Jessi, Rachel, and Shiloh at Fusion Creative Works for making this story look good.

About the Author

She founded Aloha Publishing in 2004 to offer anyone with a powerful idea the opportunity to write and publish a high-quality book. Since that time, the team at Aloha has helped hundreds of writers and non-writers become authors with the essence of Aloha—which is love, joy, compassion, and giving. The Hawaiian word Aloha means "breath of God."

Maryanna is a coffee lover and visionary who enjoys the mountains and rivers of Idaho yet it's any beach that captures her heart. She has authored nine books over her professional career and has consulted on or published more than 400 titles.

She was very close with her grandmother, Mary Oppel, who is the subject of this book. She purchased a beautiful house in Boise's North End for the final years of her grandmother's life so she could live close to the people and places she loved so much. What Maryanna cherishes most is what she learned from her grandmother about loving Jesus and loving people.